10 Laws of Power for Entrepreneurs

Yura Bryant

To every entrepreneur who is hustling to make their vision a reality.

Introduction

Power. Transformation. Entrepreneur. Successful. These words form an ambitious image in your mind that makes you envision your life transitioning to a new level of existence. Power means that you possess strength and have earned the respect of others. Transformation represents your life evolving into a better reality. Entrepreneur defines you exploiting market opportunities to build your own empire. Successful describes your ability to accomplish your goals and live a lifestyle above the average existence. Now think about the imagery produced within your mind from the description of these four words. Wouldn't it be wonderful if all these words were used to describe you?

Imagine people being inspired by your life. Your ambition to succeed and persistence to be great provides the motivation for others to hold themselves to a higher standard. They use your story of rising from humble beginnings to mind-blowing success as inspiration to keep focused on their own goals of success. You're the successful entrepreneur who is being featured in Entrepreneur, Forbes, and Inc. You've accomplished what only a few have done and is constantly being recognized for your unrelenting desire to win and ability to execute your goals.

Damn! Wouldn't that be a nice life to live? Unfortunately, this dream-like life will only remain a wishful desire for the majority of people wanting to make this life their reality. So the question I have for you is, "Do you have the ability to bring the burning desire for success that currently only lives within your mind into existence?"

Of course, you will respond YES with great conviction. You wouldn't think otherwise because you strongly believe in

Introduction

your ability to become a successful entrepreneur. But while your initial enthusiasm is great, it doesn't guarantee success will attach itself to you. Truthfully, every aspiring entrepreneur is enthusiastic about the thought of being successful but most will fail miserably at their attempt to produce the results they have in their mind.

You can ask the countless number of people who have experienced a failed business about the difficulties of entrepreneurship. They'll tell you that it's impossible to just wake up one day and build a successful business overnight. If you do come at entrepreneurship with this type of approach you're guaranteed to fail because you're operating based on the misguided belief of instant success. Success doesn't just happen because of how great you think you are -- even if you worked so hard for two hours while wasting the rest of your day away. Yes, many people do think that they deserve to be successful for doing absolutely nothing.

Quite honestly, I'm tired of hearing and seeing people who have all these high hopes about being an entrepreneur when they're really just wasting their breath. I hate seeing Facebook post from the same people about how they're going to be successful when they continuously do more talking than actual work. They do the same speech every year and they're situation never changes, which makes me want to say, "Stop bullshitting yourself!"

I'm very candid and real, which is why I never attempt to sugarcoat anything -- no matter how disheartening the cold truth can sound. I must give you real information without a filter even if it may taste bad in your mouth when reading the words. Don't take my grim words as an attempt to scare

Introduction

you away from moving forward with your entrepreneurial pursuit. Take it as a challenge. The challenge I'm proposing is for you to be great!

Being an entrepreneur is not for everybody. Yes, this book was specifically written to mold your thoughts and behaviors towards producing successful entrepreneurial results. But realistically, only a few individuals reading this book will actually apply the information given within it -- no matter if I guarantee success will be produced if you implement the knowledge I give you. Hopefully I'm wrong about this statement. The reason I say this, though is because most people are too lazy to put in the work to become a better version of themselves. That's why mediocrity is so abundant in today's world. It would seem that the overwhelming amount of average people occupying the earth points to the fact that success is based on pure luck. Only a lazy fool would hold such an opinion!

Reading words to only overlook the meaning of why they have been arranged in their particular sequence is what the average person does. They lack comprehension skills which is needed to succeed in the world of entrepreneurship. You must read the words I'm writing with the intent to comprehend the lessons being presented and then apply the wisdom you gain to your own entrepreneurial journey. This simple but very important process is the first step towards attracting success as an entrepreneur.

I wish I knew how to comprehend and apply knowledge earlier in my own entrepreneur journey. My inability to do so led to me wasting nearly 10 years of my life struggling as an entrepreneur. I was frustrated seeing how other entrepreneurs

Introduction

around me were experiencing great success while I could not even make a damn sale. Hell, I didn't even know how to sell. It was embarrassing, frustrating, soul crushing, and I felt like a fraud for even talking about entrepreneurship when I didn't even feel worthy of being called an entrepreneur.

It took me years to realize what I was doing wrong. Instead of doing the same bullshit over and over again, I had to step back to analyze how successful entrepreneurs operate. Once I did that my results started to drastically improve. Now I want to share this information with you. I want to cut your learning curve in half so that you can produce successful results in significantly less time than it took me.

So if I come off as harsh, it's only because my goal is to make sure you thoroughly understand the entrepreneurial process that leads to prosperous results. I'm not here to sell you a dream about how easy it'll be for you to become a successful entrepreneur in a week or month just because you imagine living such a lifestyle every day and night. If that were the case then the word failure wouldn't even exist. It does, though and I will do my best to help you avoid it if you're truly committed to learning and applying the 10 laws detailed in this book.

What I have provided within these pages are 10 laws that cover mindset, actions, and strategy. Being a successful entrepreneur requires you to incorporate these three components into your process since they work together to give you a higher probability of producing successful results. The 10 laws work in combination with one another to produce massive results since you're applying multiple actions with each step you take. My goal for when you're

Introduction

done reading this book is to implement the 10 laws into your own operations and watch as you build your authority and increase your business profits.

This will only be achieved if you read this book with the intent to learn how to truly operate as a successful entrepreneur and not with the hope of learning some get rich quick 'techniques'. You'll definitely be disappointed if the hope of learning that bullshit is what made you interested in reading this book. I take pride in my reputation and I don't need it stained by being labeled as a scam artist who manipulates fools with lofty dreams.

Remember, you must read with the intent to understand so that you can actually implement the strategies for success that are being given to you. Be receptive to having your current thoughts and entrepreneurial process challenged and corrected. Letting go of your ego will allow you to position yourself for success, instead of wanting it handed to you because you believe you're entitled to it. You're not owed anything. The success that you want so badly must be earned. A year or two after you're done reading this book, I want to hear from you about how the knowledge you gained helped you completely transform your struggling entrepreneur existence into one full of success and wealth.

Are you ready to learn how to produce massive results? This seems like a dumb question to ask when I think about it but it must be asked because most people aren't truly serious about escaping their average life. If that's the case for you, there's no need to continue reading and wasting more time than you already have if you're not going to apply the knowledge I'm giving to you. Only move forward if you're going to allow

Introduction

these laws to govern your entrepreneurial process. Since my stern rant has been given, let's dig further into the mindset and actions that make a successful entrepreneur.

What's the Separation Between Mediocrity and Success?

Everyday there's someone who wakes up with the desire to be an entrepreneur. They're intrigued by the successful lifestyle entrepreneurship provides to those who have seem to mastered its complex nature. They have aspirations of creating a successful business in order to finally gain financial freedom in a world where they feel their control is non-existent . These are the individuals who eagerly consume as much content as possible about the fundamentals of building a successful business. They become an avid student of entrepreneurship, hoping the information they devour will translate into them creating their own thriving enterprise. While your initial aspiration to be successful is great, what happens to it once your reality doesn't match your dreams?

This must be addressed because an overwhelming number of entrepreneurs are struggling to make their businesses successful. They once had the lofty ambitions an aspiring entrepreneur uses as their motivation to start a business but now they're happy to just make ends meet every month. Every day is a stressful grind for them. They don't have enough existing customers to support their business, which means they struggle to acquire new customers because they don't know how to communicate their business's value. They're definitely not living the successful entrepreneurial lifestyle they once envisioned. The never-ending question

Introduction

running through their mind is if they should just give up and get a 'real job'.

Successful entrepreneurs are the inspiration for those who want to pursue the path of entrepreneurship because their reality is not merely a dream. These are ambitious individuals who are living life on their own terms because they took the risk to build a business that provides them with real freedom instead of settling with the 'security' of employment. How many people do you personally know who are actually free to live life as they choose? Maybe one or two individuals, if any at all.

The ability to create this type of lifestyle that the average person will never live is dependent on being a producer for consumers -- consumers being the average person. This truth seems so simple when written with only a few words but the majority of people continue to struggle with thinking and acting as a producer but will swear that their desire for success is their ultimate goal. Clearly there's a disconnection occurring somewhere and for whatever reason, people continue making the same mistakes over and over again, failing to attract success in their life. The 10 laws provided will help explain why these mistakes occur and how to correct these issues.

So what is it that separates successful entrepreneurs from struggling entrepreneurs? Is it luck, timing, or maybe it's personal connections? There has to be some secret information that only a few individuals are privileged to know that they keep to themselves. That can be the only explanation for why only a very few entrepreneurs are wildly successful, while the majority of entrepreneurs seem to be

Introduction

dealing with the uphill battle of trying to grow their businesses. Honestly, seeing others win while you continue to lose can be very agonizing to endure. It makes you question why all your hard work continues to go unnoticed.

An important fact to understand is that entrepreneurship is a process. The results produced from this process are dependent on your thoughts, actions, and habits. These three components combine together to become your behavior that influences the reality you experience as an entrepreneur. What's fascinating is that so many entrepreneurs don't recognize this fact, which causes them to ignore the major role that their own actions play in creating the failure they experience. They assume that wanting success is all that is required to produce a successful business, as if strategy and hustle aren't a part of the equation. If that were the case then every dreamer in this world would be living out the fantasy in their head.

What's extremely troubling is that so many people pursued entrepreneurship based upon the fantasy they imagined would come into fruition if they just started a business. The truth about a fantasy is that there isn't much work required to produce it within your mind. A business on the other hand requires for an individual to match their big imagination with massive actions. This is where the fine line between struggle and success is established. Therefore, maybe it's a valid opinion to assume that most people who have hopes to succeed as an entrepreneur are simply too lazy to produce the big results they only get to experience in their mind. This leads to them having the foolish belief that they're entitled to success. This silly type of thinking is what makes failure

Introduction

become an inevitable outcome for their entrepreneurial journey.

I feel like I would just be making a broad generalization of many entrepreneurs who are struggling without giving a rebuttal to the previous statement. Feelings of entitlement and being lazy aren't the overwhelming reason for why most entrepreneurs who struggle are in their difficult predicament. The real reason is because they simply don't understand how to create an effective process that leads them towards their desired destination. This lack of knowledge means that a lot of spur of the moment decisions are being made, which results in the inability to create the positive momentum of consistency needed to build towards success. We'll come back to inconsistency later in the book to discuss how it negates success.

When you become an entrepreneur, you have to reject the mediocre mindset and behavior that infects the average person. The average person willingly accepts mediocrity as their standard of living, allowing this disease to control how they operate in the world. They want wealth, success, and power but do more talking than producing. These are the people who are frustrated and envious when they see successful people who actually enjoy the life they live. Excuses begin to fill their head explaining why that person has found success in their life and they haven't. What they fail to acknowledge is the fact that their thoughts , habits, and behavior is what directly influences their current position in life. They're not putting out the right type of energy or creating the effective actions that attract success. Trying to force the underwhelming behavior of mediocrity into a

Introduction

successful entrepreneurial venture is impossible. Yet, people will continue to make this very mistake because they foolishly think entrepreneurship is an easy gateway to wealth.

Many people are currently in the pursuit of being a successful entrepreneur and the vast majority of them will fail at their attempt. Why is the failure rate of small businesses so high? It's high because failure tends to correspond with self-sabotaging behavior that denies an individual the ability to succeed.

It makes you wonder if some individuals are just born to be entrepreneurs, while the vast majority of people are meant to only be employees. An argument supporting this opinion can be made since employees are needed to sustain a business's operations, which means entrepreneurs can't exceed the available workforce. But that's only glossing over the real reason for why only a small number of individuals succeed in entrepreneurship.

The truth is just that some people are better at comprehending how the entrepreneurial process works. They know how to combine together the most important elements of entrepreneurship to create successful ventures and businesses. The majority of struggling entrepreneurs don't understand how this connection works because they allow themselves to become distracted by actions that don't facilitate growth. This means they're not focused on making money, they rather play like they're an entrepreneur.

Want to know an open secret? The two most important functions in entrepreneurship are marketing and sales. The

Introduction

most important criteria in regards to these functions is the value provided by your offer. Focusing on these three areas of your entrepreneurial process will lead to your business achieving exponential growth.

That's pretty straightforward, right? It seems that way but remember that entrepreneurship is a process involving many different moving pieces. You're dealing with customers, competition, and unpredictable circumstances that you can't always control. Therefore, you'll have to learn how to create as much control as possible in order to produce successful results. And honestly, the constant battle for control is very draining both mentally and physically. You must be built to go to war everyday if your goal is to come out on the winning side.

This is why the 10 laws enclosed in this book were created. They're focused on teaching you how to establish your position of power through strategic thinking and effective actions. This allows you to create a strategy that actually produces results, rather than just wasting your time due to your own inconsistent behavior. Time is too valuable of a resource to waste, so the goal is to learn how to maximize this precious asset as best as possible.

When you're intent on maximizing your actions, you set yourself up to operate on a level beyond the capacity of the average human being. Your work ethic increases as a result but you also work smarter as you work harder, which is one of the keys to becoming successful. The benefit of understanding how to do both at the same time is what leads to an explosion in opportunities and wealth, instead of enduring the misery of a dead business.

Introduction

As you progress further along in this book, you'll start to recognize that the 10 laws are common sense lessons for anyone calling themselves an entrepreneur. Sadly, this isn't the case because most people make entrepreneurship more difficult than it needs to be. The entrepreneurial process becomes manageable when you break down the big picture into smaller pieces that are easier to handle. The laws within this book represent the most important aspects of entrepreneurship broken down into 10 manageable pieces. This helps you view entrepreneurship as a process of many different pieces combined over time to work together, instead of one big event that immediately happens.

Take a moment to think about what you want to achieve as an entrepreneur before reading any further. How will you gain possession of these dreams that currently only live within your head? You'll do it by following the laws given in this book! Once you come to the realization that being successful and wealthy is the only option for your life, you'll learn how to think and act strategically to make your desire a reality.

Are you ready to transform the trajectory of your entrepreneurial journey? The journey towards success won't be easy, but it'll be well worth your unrelenting effort to bring it into fruition when you're actively enjoying a lifestyle most people will only experience in their dreams.

Law I

Law I: Have a Vision Guiding Your Actions

Vision provides you with the ability to know what choices are available to you so that you can make the right decision about what's the best course of action to take to accomplish your goals. Without the ability to see, your movement in the world becomes severely limited because you're prone to being blindsided without warning as to what is coming your way. The sense of confinement this deficiency creates forces you to seek solace in a safe, risk free environment because your ability to survive in a world full of challenges is severely limited.

Think about how a lack of vision negatively affects your ability to prosper as an entrepreneur. The distractions of building a business can blind you to the purpose of what your real objective is as an entrepreneur... **to make money!** When you give non-money making activities as much importance as money making activities, you make it impossible for your business to generate a consistent flow of sales. This causes you to continuously work in your business instead of working on your business, which is asinine because you're trying to make your business perfect instead of generating interest from your target market to secure customers. This mistake happens because you haven't created a strategy that is solely focused on the task of making money. But with a strategic blueprint in place, you eliminate distractions that blind you from seeing the true health of your business.

The health of your business is something that you must scrutinize over every single day. Knowing this status helps you understand how you're currently operating so you can

Law I

determine how to improve your own personal actions and your business operations to improve its performance. Unfortunately, many entrepreneurs never do this necessary assessment because they aren't obsessed with their business's health. Not having the ability to understand how your business is performing means you're consistently doing the wrong things, which means a lot of actions are being done that don't align together to produce growth.

An Unplanned Destination Leads to Being Permanently Lost

Trust me when I tell you I know how frustrating it is to try to build a business without a vision. You desperately want results for your efforts but are constantly met with a brick wall no matter what you do. The reason this occurs is because you're operating without a defined process that's supposed to gradually build up over time to make any type of resistance to your vision difficult to succeed.

This is why a vision is important because it sets the course of actions implemented within your strategy. As you keep moving forward and working your strategy, you gain more exposure and credibility for your business. To make it this far, though you need to be consistent and have the patience to see the process all the way through. These two attributes can only be possessed when a strategy is in place to keep you focused on achieving the desired vision for your business.

If you keep bumping your head against the wall it means that the actions you're putting into motion need to be changed immediately. Finding out why the issues are occurring is dependent on you outlining your desired destination, which

Law 1

will help you develop the actions that correspond with your goals. When you know where you want to go, your actions are backed by purpose. Purpose led actions work to reduce the time you waste, while increasing your daily output. Now you'll be moving forward consistently at a rapid pace, instead of remaining stagnant or moving backwards and further away from completing your goals.

Winners Know Where They're Going

The entrepreneurs who are experiencing an abundance of prosperity are those who understand that a successful business cannot be built based on guessing what your next move is going to be. Every course of action you take needs to be based upon producing the best outcome that leads you closer to your desired vision. You can only do this by comparing what you did previously and readjusting your actions to produce better results. This keeps you completely focused on accomplishing your current goals so that you can continue to set new goals to be achieved. Therefore, you're never satisfied with your past success because your vision for what you must become is beyond a few small wins and the praise you receive from other people.

This is why entrepreneurs such as Steve Jobs, Bill Gates, and Elon Musk built great companies that are recognized around the world. Their visions went beyond the small imaginations of onlookers who marveled at their past and present accomplishments. They understand that in order to remain successful, they had to recognize that the future must always be worked towards in the present day. Once you forget to focus on the future you become the past.

Law I

Take the time to study the average person to understand how they see and operate within the world. You'll notice they're confined to mediocrity because they don't see beyond such an existence. Sure, they see successful people and want the same for themselves but they never visualize themselves actually working towards their desire for success. There's always some type of excuse that they use to validate why it hasn't entered their life.

This is why having a vision is so important because it sets the precedent for how you conduct your actions. You hold yourself to a higher standard by being accountable for your actions, which makes you 100% responsible for the success you gain or the failure you earn. No excuses can be used to validate your reason for failing to succeed. You either make shit happen or you shut up and find comfort with mediocrity!

You Must be Obsessed with the Hustle to Attract Success

You're either going to be obsessed with the dream in your head or with actually producing real results that allow you to experience your vision in reality. Too many individuals who are trying to become entrepreneurs fall in love with the thought of success but aren't committed to the process it takes to get there. You have to be obsessed the hustle because that's what pushes you through the challenges that are constantly presented to hold you back. When you're obsessed with winning, you'll find a solution to any problem because succeeding is your only option. It won't just be handed to you, you have to reach out and take it.

Law I

I've never met a successful person who earned their status through pure luck. They made a plan and worked their strategy to execution by eliminating all the distractions around them. You achieve this for yourself when your vision dominates your thoughts, forcing you to do everything in your power to bring it into fruition. Therefore, it boils down to how bad you really want to see yourself succeed.

Transforming your vision into a reality is simply dependent on applying effective actions. The difficult part of this process is determining what actions actually move you forward in achieving your goals. But finding out how to get from point A to point B is less difficult when you know exactly where you're going. Plus, success cannot find your path if you don't give it the opportunity to know you're looking for it. Set your vision, believe in it, work hard towards it, and you'll begin to radiate the energy that attracts success to you.

Law II

Law II: Back Up Talk with Actions

If only we could become successful and wealthy just because we said it out of our mouths. Life would be so simple with the ease of being able to literally speak your thoughts into existence by merely mentioning them and not having to do any actual work. It's a great thing that success doesn't come so easily because a person doesn't deserve to partake in the wonders granted by success just because of having the word success constantly come out of their mouth.

It might come across as harsh to make such a statement but it's very true. What you wish to have doesn't matter if your work ethic doesn't exceed your words. For every 100 people talking about how they want to be successful, maybe only 10 of those people are actually putting in the work to bring their dreams into fruition. That's only 10%, which perfectly sums up why the average person vastly outnumbers those recognized as successful.

It's quite strange that people find it hard to back up their words with actions but not necessarily mind boggling. Humans are naturally lazy. We tend to seek the easy way out of hard situations if the option is presented to us. Who wouldn't take the easiest route available that presents no resistance and doesn't make you uncomfortable? A person who understands that success requires the sacrifice of time and effort wouldn't. Also, take into account that we live in a world today that provides us with so many distractions that appeal to our lazy nature. It's no wonder why it's so difficult to concentrate on the goal of attaining success when your

Law II

mind is focused on garbage made to keep you entertained and mentally weak.

That's just a very poor excuse to use, though. If you can't put your goals before self-gratification then you'll never gain success. All that talk about how you'll be the next Bill Gates is meaningless if you spend all your free time watching T.V., playing video games, and going out every single night blowing your money on frivolous things. You're wasting time on non-productive activities, while giving very little, if any attention to your stated goals. Therefore, wherever you concentrate the majority of your time and energy reflects the state of life that you'll live.

Your Thoughts Must be Supported with Effective Actions

Entrepreneurship is supposed to dominate your life -- meaning consume the thoughts which influence your actions. No successful entrepreneur earned their position among the elite without putting in hours upon hours of work every single day, including weekends. Knowing this as being fact, you must eliminate the bullshit behavior that currently exist in your life and focus on what brings your vision into reality.

As an entrepreneur, you have to know how to be brutally efficient with your time in order to get the most out of each day. It's incredible how people assume they can just put their goals off until the next day, as if the unpredictability of life and taking advantage of the right time aren't factors to consider. From the very moment you say you have a goal that needs to be accomplished, you need to create a strategy that moves you closer to accomplishing your goal. You have to

19

Law II

behave like a madman who's obsessed with the fascination that dominates his thoughts, which over time influences his resulting behavior. This obsession will make him look crazy from the viewpoint of the person who doesn't understand his driving motivation. But these opinions don't matter to him because he knows what he must accomplish to relieve his mental anguish.

We live in a society today where social media provides you with an outlet to make huge announcements to your followers in order to make you feel empowered in that moment. I know this from first-hand experience because I've been guilty of making proclamations in the past that I never put actions behind. You may be able to cover up your bullshit for a short while with the gift of gab, but eventually you'll be exposed for being a fraud when nothing you say ever materializes.

The old saying is that *actions speak louder than words.* This statement refers to accountability. All individuals are accountable for his or her actions. Therefore, no excuse is acceptable for why you can talk all day about wanting to be successful but don't put in the effort to actually earn the reward you seek. Your lack of hustle is the complete opposite of your big talk. But you also have to be careful about where you allocate your time and energy. Focusing on the wrong activities can severely set you back, forcing you to work 10x harder to make up for the time you wasted.

Here's a bit of advice: with the end-goal in mind, create the initiatives that will gradually move you towards accomplishing your vision. Implementing a step-by-step process eliminates the mistakes caused by trying to become

Law II

an overnight success. Trying to accomplish ten things at one time is a recipe for disaster because you're not dedicating enough time to each action for them to flesh out and become effective. Frustration is the only result produced from operating in this manner because you're denied the ability to see how the entrepreneurial process actually works.

You start building towards your desired vision when you operate with purpose instead of just doing what comes to your mind at the moment. Relying on scattered thoughts to guide your actions will lead to you being inconsistent. And remember, you must be brutally efficient with your time and effective with your actions to come into possession of your aspirations.

Creating a Winning Strategy

No war has ever been won without preparing for each battle with tactics that support the overall strategy. What you have to determine is the best tactics that will help you succeed in both the short-term and long-term. Just focusing on the short-term will eventually lead to stagnation since your actions aren't developed to reinforce one another for continual growth. When both the short and long-term are planned for, you maximize your actions, which positions you to succeed in a shorter amount of time.

Is it better to accomplish your goals in 5 years or 15 years, considering that you originally planned for completion in 10 years? Of course the shorter amount of time is the preferred choice but you must first learn how to make small actions add up to big accomplishments in a relatively short amount of time.

Law II

You do this by defining your vision, listing out the goals that will achieve your vision, and establishing the actions that align together to accomplish your goals. Now break this information down into manageable pieces by year, quarter, month, week, and day. Doing so develops your consistency, which continuously pushes you closer to your desired destination. This allows you to analyze your progression to determine what actions are working and which aren't producing results. You quickly eliminate the time wasting activities and put more energy and resources into those that are working. This establishes a system that combines efficiency with effectiveness, allowing you to significantly maximize your actions to produce bigger results.

The positive reinforcement provided by progression is a stimulant that makes you work harder as you realize that what you're doing is paying off. It's only a matter of time until you accomplish your end-goal. Therefore, you keep pushing and pushing until you experience your breakthrough.

Execute or Perish

While it's very important that you create the strategy, you must demand execution from yourself or else your vision will die. There are so many people in this world who have great ideas, create plans around those ideas, but never complete the puzzle by executing the plan they devised. That's mental torture to just keep a dream confined to your mind when it's clawing to be brought into existence. Many people have the problem of trying to create the perfect plan that has to be executed at the perfect time. Perfect doesn't exist. While you're waiting for the perfect opportunity, someone else with

Law II

the same idea as you is grabbing the attention of your target market you refuse to go after.

During prehistoric times hunters led and were celebrated because they ferociously and meticulously stalked their prey. If they weren't successful, they starved and died, along with the people dependent on their success. Only the strongest and smartest fared well. The weak were dependent on the hunters and were subject to their rules because they weren't capable of providing for themselves.

The world still operates in this manner, only slightly more sophisticated. The keywords that are now used to describe this type of relationship are **producer** and **consumer.** A producer creates the products and services that the consumer purchases. The continual consumption by the consumer makes the producer wealthy, while the consumer typical lives paycheck to paycheck and under considerable debt. The actions taken by the producer to become a provider for the consumer enables that individual to live a successful lifestyle because they actively pursued the economic idea that was present in their mind.

Opportunities are presented to all of us but it takes the initiative to exploit these openings before they're closed off to us to develop them into big gains. Everybody has aspirations to be successful but the implementation of effective actions that lead to results being produced is where only a few succeed. This is why the failure rate for entrepreneurs is incredibly high. Most aspiring entrepreneurs don't know how to think and act beyond the average capacity. You have to raise your level of performance if you want to go where you've never been before.

Law II

Become Results Driven

We live in a society today where failure is celebrated. It's quite odd, honestly. Yes, I recognize nobody is perfect because I'm certainly not. Therefore, among the wins has to be some losses. But who the hell really feels satisfaction when they fail?

It's true that you learn from your mistakes that created the defeat you experienced. But entrepreneurs are hungry sharks savagely swimming in the ocean in search for their next meal. The desperation brought on by the desire to win makes the window for failure very small. When this is the reality that exist for you, producing results becomes incredibly important.

Your focus on success must be completely unwavering. Eliminate all distractions that will detract away from your ability to be resolute towards your established purpose. This means eliminating people, places, and things that subtract from you rather than adding value to you. You must be selfish about your success because nobody else gives a damn about the challenge of your journey towards it until you finally make it and can be of benefit to them.

Taking control of your success will only occur with you being ruthless with your actions. Say what you want about Donald Trump but he was ruthless with his campaign strategy to secure his occupancy in the White House. He tapped into the emotions of his base and stroked their ideologies to secure their loyal support. Their blind loyalty meant they ignored any mistakes he made because he made them feel as if held the same beliefs as them. Trump placed

Law II

himself in one of the most powerful positions in the world by listening and acting upon the information he received from his target base. With this insight, he portrayed himself as the champion for America who would restore it to its former glory.

Your approach to entrepreneurship has to be just as efficient and ruthless when it comes to your own success. Discover the information and tactics that will help you secure a victory and put tremendous actions behind them. Determine what's going on in the industry you plan to operate within -- currently and future developments. Learn about the influencers who dominate that marketplace so you can get to know them. Find out what customers think about the current options available to them so you can learn how to make improvements. With this thorough research, you'll be able to create a strategy of actions that produces results because it's devised based on real insight rather than mere assumptions.

Law III

Law III: Think Like a Consumer

Too many people jump into entrepreneurship thinking about how much money they can make instead of focusing on how to provide the best products and services to their customers. When you're blinded by money, you put your own selfish needs before those of your customers. This isn't to say that you shouldn't focus on making as much money as possible. I chose to be an entrepreneur because I want financial freedom and I know you have the same goal. But your business's finances correlate with how well you serve your customers.

If you fail to put the customer first, you'll never create a consistent flow of cash coming into your business. Product quality and customer service are two things that you must always ensure exceed your customer's expectations. People talk and pissed customers tend to share their bad experiences with your business more so than satisfied customers. Therefore, you need to control the narrative so that you nor your business is ever perceived as unsavory in the marketplace.

Your ability to control people's perception about your business is dependent on how well you structure the interaction they have with it. What is it that you want your customers to experience with your business on a consistent basis? When you can answer this question, you're able to create a business culture that promotes positive communication and interaction, which leads to happy customers.

Think of the brand that Apple has created which has developed a cult following unlike any other company

Law III

operating in today's marketplace. The reason the company was able to build such a magnetic brand is because Steve Jobs understood that exceeding customer's expectations would position Apple as a dominant industry leader. To accomplish this same feat for your business, though you must get inside the mind of your customer and see your brand through their eyes.

What do Your Customers Really Want?

Creating a business based upon your opinions about what your customers wants instead of facts is a sure way to fail. Arrogance and ignorance have been the cause of casualty for many businesses. Trying to force the customer to purchase your product without understanding their needs and wants is very foolish. If you're not aware of their pain points to create a solution that eliminates their problems then they will see no use for your offer.

Entrepreneurship is a mixture of psychology and sociology, which means you play the role of a therapist who builds a community around your business. You're dealing with people on an individual level and different subsets of a demographic that fit within your target market. Therefore, you have to know how to communicate in an effective manner that helps you better serve your customers. Remember, communication is more than just talking. Great communication is dependent on you being a good listener who can effectively decipher the information given to you to produce a mutually beneficial outcome for you and your customers.

You must know the thoughts, motivations, and insecurities of your customers so that you can create the product or service

Law III

they must have to bring peace or growth within their life. This means you have to envision yourself as the customer who's interacting with your business and vetting your value against the competition. How would you honestly grade yourself based on how well you communicate with your customers and the value provided by your offer? This honest examination allows you to improve your communication process so that you become better at attracting and retaining customers and so you can improve any deficiencies with your product or service.

There's many different ways that you can gain better insight about your customers. This includes creating surveys, conducting focus groups, asking for their feedback after purchasing your product or service, and viewing their social media conversations about your business. With this information, you can learn their likes and dislikes about your product or service to improve it and position your offer as the most desirable option available to be purchased.

The one thing you have to do is be creative about the product or service you want to deliver to the marketplace. When you're too similar to the established market leaders, you'll lose out because they have more credibility and clout than you have as a new entry into the marketplace. But never believe that the market leaders of today will forever hold their dominant positions. Market disruption can always occur by making an existing offer appear more attractive by applying your own unique approach.

Take services such as Airbnb and Uber for examples of how disruption works. Just five years ago, when traveling to a distant location a hotel was pretty much your only option for

housing unless staying with family or friends. A taxi was
how you could get from one location to another if you didn't
have a car of your own and wanted to avoid using the bus or
subway. Now the sharing economy has completely changed
the dynamics of both these industries that once seemed to be
the only reliable source customers trusted.

This is also happening with Fintech companies that are
becoming more attractive alternatives to banks. PayPal was
one of the first fintech companies on the scene but we now
have Bitcoin, acting as a form of cryptic, digital currency.
Kabbage on the other hand, is a platform to get small
business financing without having to deal with the drawn out
process of a traditional bank loan. These type of companies
are popping up because customers have real problems with
the strict policies banks have instituted despite these financial
institutions being the ones that orchestrated the economic
meltdown caused by the issues they're now trying to police.
It's viewed as a double standard because they gained from
their destructive behavior and now want to implement
restrictions for the average person when they never restricted
themselves.

You can create disruption yourself if you listen to your
customers and think of a creative solution that satisfies their
needs by being more convenient than the existing option.
Making the lives of your customers easier means you'll
always be in demand because consumers have been spoiled
to the point of being lazy. Cater to their lazy nature and you'll
reap the rewards for your ability to provide for their need to
consume without having to deal with difficulties.

Law III

The Psychology of Pricing

The correct price to charge is a tricky choice for many entrepreneurs to make because they're not sure if they're overcharging or undercharging. This lack of clarity usually leads to the wrong decision being made since it's based on assumptions. Two issues are the reason for why this problem occurs. Not knowing the value of your offer and failure to understand the price sensitivity of your customer base. These are two crucial factors that must be known with surety to create the most rewarding outcome for you as the producer.

Know this: sales do not always equal profit. Low pricing means that you have to sale large quantities of your product or services to meet and exceed your business's expenses. This means you're chasing the dollar making pennies per sale, instead of bringing in the dollar tenfold per sale.

Determining how to set your prices is dependent on a couple of different variables. This includes: customer demographics, perceived value of your offer, supply and demand, and unique selling proposition. For many entrepreneurs, charging a low price seems like the best way to attract customers but it comes at a steep cost. Unless you're Wal-Mart, you can't win with a lowest price strategy. You don't have hundreds of millions of customers who purchase from your business everyday to bring in the revenue to support this strategy. Big companies exploit this type of strategy to force small businesses to close their doors. Therefore, this pricing approach is only doing them a favor because you're hurting yourself. Plus, when you finally realize that your prices are too low, it's hard to raise them because your existing

Law III

customers will disappear. They're not loyal to your business. They're just loyal to the convenience of your low prices.

To avoid putting yourself in this hole, you need to create a customer profile that gives you a framework of your ideal customer. This profile will give you a blueprint of your customer's persona and purchasing behavior, which gives you context on how to market and sale to them based upon your pricing. Well, that's if you're focusing on price as your sales strategy, which shouldn't be your approach.

It's more beneficial to focus on the value you offer. When you can effectively communicate the satisfaction provided to the customer by your product or service, they tend to overlook price in favor of gratification. The stimulus produced from the brain when it's intoxicated by happiness can sway an individual to make the decision that keeps that happy euphoria going. Who cares about how much something cost when you're happy with what you purchased, right? If your customers hold this mindset then don't be afraid to feed their eagerness to consume your products and services. Consumers are always going to spend money as long as there's a producer around to take their money. Be the producer that satisfies one of their particular needs and get paid well for doing so.

Branding Power

Apple is notorious for using their powerful brand to make tons of money. How much is the iPhone X? $1,000+ for a phone that has some updated features and a slightly different design. There are many Apple loyalist who have decided to forgo buying the phone due to its price (so they say). But you

Law III

can be sure the phone will be purchased in large quantities because Apple's brand prestige is incredibly strong. Is Apple trying to find out just how powerful the brand they have built actually is? That may be the case if demand for their products continue to rise despite price increasing at the same.

Building a powerful brand isn't something that just happens a month after you open up for business. It takes a lot of time, effort, and trial and error to understand how to position your brand for long-term success. The point of branding is to distinguish your product from the competition, which gives the consumer an indication about which provider they should purchase from. This tells you that perception is highly important when it comes to the decisions that a customer makes when having to choose between 2-3 different brands that offer the same product. The brand that is decided upon is the one that resonates well with the customer's lifestyle and needs.

The first step to building a powerful brand is identifying the value being provided to your customers. Knowing exactly how you make their lives easier means that you can effectively communicate why they need to purchase what you're providing. Notice I didn't say selling. Even though you're selling a product or service, you have to view yourself as a provider who caters to the needs of your customers. A provider seeks to nurture the relationship so that it can grow stronger with each interaction. The goal is to make the customer understand you're more concerned about them as an individual instead of the money they're spending. Even though being a consumer is about the exchange of money for a product or service, that individual wants to believe their

Law III

patronage is appreciated beyond how much money they spend. Show appreciation for them being a customer and it'll be reciprocated with their loyalty.

Creating value for your customers is a combination of your product or service providing solutions to problems and emotional therapy. Money well spent is viewed as an investment rather than an expense for happy customers. When other people observe how happy a customer is when spending their money with your business, they want to understand what is the cause for so much enthusiasm by spending their own money to find out. The repeated cycle of curious interest that leads to money being spent with your business builds a brand that has great recognition in its industry, creating a significant position of power. Therefore, you must understand these keys for making your brand attractive so it can continue to develop and grow with each customer purchase.

Brand recognition must be viewed as a resource similar to capital. This resource can be leveraged for capital investment, partnerships, and emerging opportunities. These possibilities are only available when your brand is seen as an asset that can help improve the position of an individual or business interested in establishing a beneficial relationship with your business. Building your brand's recognition is easier today than it was in the past. The advantages and access provided by social media allows for you to interact with your target market around the clock and on a more personal level. There are people who have leveraged their YouTube channel into their own shows on powerhouse networks like HBO, appearances on radio, and television interviews. Individuals who have hundreds of thousands to millions of followers on Instagram are making 6 figures from promoting advertiser's products on their pages and selling their own products and services. The opportunities available in today's world are abundant but you only attract them by having a strong brand.

You need to decide what your brand represents and craft a message to communicate this to the world. This message must remain consistent so that your brand is viewed as authentic and not constantly changing to fit the latest trend. Pound your brand's message into the minds of your audience with every interaction they have with you and your business. You don't have to say the same words every time when communicating your message. You can say the same message in a variety of ways to drive home your point so that people know exactly what your brand stands for. The goal is to make your audience automatically associate your brand with the product or service you provide.

Nike represents athletic performance. McDonalds is the leader of burgers and fries. Apple provides cool, innovative technology that you must have. Each company creates their own brand distinction so that the consumer can distinguish their value from their competitors. Your brand must cultivate an attractive image that resonates among consumers as the go-to place for the particular need you serve. This is how you create loyal followers who develop into a cult following.

It's all About the Experience

What are you selling to your customers? You might think it's products or a service but you're really selling an experience.

Law III

From the initial point of engagement to the interaction after the purchase is made, your business is constantly under the microscope to be scrutinized. Unfortunately, there are people who want to see you fail just because you operate a business and will find any little issue to make bigger than it really is -- even if they're the sole cause of said issue. This is why it's important to create an experience that's too hard for people to not enjoy. When you make the customer's satisfaction the ultimate goal, it's extremely hard for them to find fault with the experience your business administers. Matter of fact, great customer experience will make your supporters defend you without question against your detractors because they know you always seek to exceed their expectations.

As mentioned, the customer experience is an on-going process that extends beyond the initial purchase. After all, you want repeat customers and not just onetime buyers. Nurturing the relationship to be fruitful is all about how well you make the customer feel wanted. You have to show high interest in your customers even when they aren't spending money. Keep the communication going, educate them about the important developments in your industry, acknowledge their loyalty to your business. Your customers should feel as if they're an integral part of your business. This means inviting them into your culture and building that culture around them.

If taking these measures seems like you're going overboard, then you're not really serious about building a successful brand. Something has to set your business apart from the competition and that separation is dependent on the connection you create with your customers. It has constantly been mentioned that emotions play a big part in the purchasing decisions that customers make. Therefore, you must make it a point to feed their emotions to increase your brand's power.

This might seem manipulative but all communication and interaction in life is supposed to produce a response. Strategic people with a goal to accomplish understand you must sway emotions in the direction you require to produce the results you want. Once again, it's about results oriented actions. Therefore, the experience you create for your customers must to lead to a specific outcome -- the continual spending of money with your business.

The purpose of an experience is to create certain feelings that lead to a desired action being taken. Whatever feelings you want your customers to associate with your brand need to be telegraphed through your messaging. The visuals and commentary you use need to create an image that reflects your brand well and highlights why people should be your customers. Lead them through a journey of feelings with words and imagery that guides them towards the desired destination you want to occur within their mind.

The experience you communicate should immerse the customer within the value your business provides. Telling a story that illustrates how you helped create a change in an existing customer's life entices them to yearn for the same experience. You must realize that visual stimulation helps people better connect with your brand. Why do you think YouTube is ranked the #2 website in the world? It's because people enjoy watching stories play out on-screen and feeling as if they're part of the experience they're viewing. Keeping

Law III

your audience entertained while at the same time educating them about the value your business provides will help make your brand standout. After all, you can't build a powerful brand if you're not recognizable.

You must remember that customers typically make their purchase decisions based upon their emotions. Being that emotions play such a big role in their decision making, you must learn how to influence their emotions for your benefit. This is how success and wealth is earned and kept by those who have attained the presence of both. The few understand that you must shape the thoughts of the masses to steer them in the direction you desire. When you know the exact thoughts of your customers, you understand how to create a sense of reality they must have within their own lives.

Law IV

Law IV: Keep the Competition Guessing

Every person in this world is in competition whether they realize it or not. The earth is becoming over-populated, which means the resources available in the world are being consumed at a rapid pace. As resources become more scarce, the ability to control the supply of resources grants immense power to those who hold such a position. Taking this into account, every move you make as an entrepreneur must be about securing a better position within your industry to dominate the marketplace. This is accomplished by being 10 steps ahead of your competitors. While they're just catching up to your last step, you're moving forward and leading the next development in your industry.

Entrepreneurship is the competition you deal with in everyday life intensified 10x. You're competing with hundreds of similar providers who want those same customers you're after. Consumers today are already cash strapped so them choosing multiple providers for the same product or service isn't a viable option. Therefore, you must find a way to standout from the other available options to become the preferred choice. To do this you must know your customers, stay ahead of the industry, and perform better than your competition. The ability to do these three things will position your business to attract more opportunities and customers, which means more money being generated to accelerate continued growth.

Law IV

Create a Competitive Advantage

Competition is all about the advantages you use to create leverage over your opposition to gain favorable positioning. A lot of entrepreneurs make the mistake of trying to compete on the same level of their competition and this is one of their biggest mistakes. Pricing is the strategy often used but that's a terrible choice because it doesn't present a big enough distinction when everyone is putting an emphasis on their prices. Taking this into account, you must determine another area where you can excel and establish firm control. This is the thing that you do so well that your competitors have an extremely hard time even performing near your level of excellence.

In the previous paragraph, price was mentioned as a preferred strategy that businesses choose to compete with. On the corporate level, McDonalds and Wal-Mart have employed this strategy for years but it is finally catching up with them. Burger King and Wendy's have a value meal to rival McDonald's dollar menu. As low-income families are stretched to the max, Wal-Mart now has to attract high-income families to help replace the loss of lower-income shoppers. Additionally, competitors such as Amazon are going after lower-income families with attractive incentives to make them abandon Wal-Mart. At the end of the day, when pricing is what you depend on as an advantage, it can easily become a liability when your competitors make their low pricing more attractive than yours.

These are billion dollar companies playing price wars, though. As a smaller business, you aren't able to compete on the level of these behemoths. You'll need to focus on customer service, product value, or extremely great branding. You're probably saying to yourself this is only three options, which means there's no way you're the only person focusing on one or all three of these criteria. You'd be surprised to learn how many people are operating businesses without caring about being excellent at something to keep their customers happy and loyal to them. They believe the fact that they're open for business is reason enough for why they should experience high demand for their products or services. This type of arrogance is why only the individuals who are focused on the needs of their customers create highly successful businesses.

Solely focusing on one area where you're great can produce massive returns on that investment. Superiority in one lane is vastly better than being only average in several areas that split your focus and effectiveness. Mastery is only gained when your focus has one primary goal to accomplish. Applying this disciplined approach to your business will help you create a competitive advantage that is very hard for your competition to compete against. Therefore, you either approach entrepreneurship with a deep desire to be the best at what you do or you accept mediocre results and shut your mouth complaining about how it's not fair that your business sucks.

Make the Future the Present

When you're not prepared to operate in the future, your present day will eventually become a failure. So many businesses have failed because their leaders were satisfied with past success, as if it would lead them far into the future. The lack of preparing for the future caused them to turn a

Law IV

blind eye to the changes occurring in their industry and how their competition was evolving. Once the shift is finally noticed, it's too late to be proactive or even react successfully. This creates a hole that is almost impossible to dig out of without a great deal of money being spent to acquire that competitor, because the option of competing is no longer available without experiencing short-term or even long-term losses.

When you're an entrepreneur, there's never a period of time when you can rest because you believe your market position is secure. If the opportunity to generate tons of money is present in your industry, people are going to try their hardest to gain control of their piece of the market share. You're dealing with hungry sharks who have no problem killing your business to help theirs succeed. When this is the mindset that is held by your competitors, you must out maneuver them at every step to remain firmly ahead.

The best way to do this is by knowing your customers and how their needs will dictate the future of your industry. The opportunities gained from such insight can be worth millions, maybe even billions if you know how to use the information collected to create a master plan that is executed with precision. The ability to create innovation is be done by simply seeing all sides of a problem to develop an absolute solution. This means your product or service completely eradicates the customer's problem or transitions their life or business to a new level of existence. When it comes down to it, the results you produce on a consistent basis are what determines your business's success.

Law IV

Never become complacent, whether you're currently experiencing success or even stalled progression. Your circumstances can change in what seems like a blink of an eye but they actually occur over time due to your daily habits. Therefore, what you do today affects the results you experience in the future. Smart entrepreneurs recognize this fact and always work to position their business to succeed well into the future.

It's all about being proactive instead of being reactive so that you can make smart decisions, rather than hasty decisions. Actions that are taken when your back is against the wall usually result in bigger loses occurring in the future because you don't thoroughly think about the pros and cons of the decision you're making.

Entrepreneurship equals business. And success in business is dependent on positioning your operations for long-term prosperity. The actions and decisions that you make today are an investment that will eventual yield a return when they mature in the future. The harvest that is produced from the seeds you planted is a reflection of how well you nurtured the development process in the early stages of growth. Your business will only go as far as you forecast it going. Plan, strategize ,execute and adjust along the way to ensure that your actions are focused on both short and long-term success. There's not too many businesses that are equipped to succeed beyond five years or even a year. Be the rare entrepreneur who creates a business that's poised to succeed for years to come, instead of experiencing a short-lived run that's remembered as a failure.

Law IV

Exceed Customer's Expectations

Let's be honest, we live in a world full of mediocrity. Mediocrity is so abundant in today's world that it's become the expected standard of performance. People just hope for the bare minimum so that their lowest expectations can be met. That's quite sad when you think about it because it means excellence isn't a standard that people are being held to, which means they no longer have to give 100% of their effort to a task.

Unfortunately, this means that there are a lot of mediocre entrepreneurs who're operating businesses that provide subpar products and service. This means two things. Lower customer expectations means that you can get by with alright products and crappy service. On the other hand, a business that focus on excellence can steal your customers away from you once word gets out about how well they treat their customers.

It's about not only about having respect for your customers but giving absolute respect to your business. You should want your business to be viewed as the best provider operating in the marketplace, instead of one that customers grudgingly choose due to convenience or low pricing. As mentioned previously, convenience and pricing can easily become an afterthought when high-quality and great value is being provided. This is why top brands dominate their industries, while their competition fights over the few consumers who are left over due to price sensitivity or location.

Law IV

This isn't meant to sound over simplified, but all it takes to win over customers is to exceed their expectations. Going over and beyond to ensure that your customer's needs are met with a wonderful experience will help your business elevate quickly in the marketplace. This is pretty much a known fact, or it should be something easy to comprehend. Yet, there are businesses that ignore the need to be excellent because they don't give a damn about being so or are just too lazy to put forth the effort that is required for excellence.

While it's frustrating to see mediocrity happen on such a rampant basis, it also presents a great opportunity for your business if you're willing to go the extra mile to separate yourself from the competition. Remember, you're dealing with people and people are generally guided by their emotions. If an individual is purchasing from you, they're establishing a relationship with your business where there's supposed to be a mutual exchange of value. It's like a marriage, which means both partners are expected to hold their end of the bargain for the union to last. Most marriages that last till death or the ones where the love feels just as strong as when it was first established. This is done by keeping the relationship fresh, instead of doing the bare minimum that barely holds the union together.

To make your customers love your brand, you need to wow them with every single interaction they have with your business. You may think this means going over the top to make a big statement but that is not the case. It means paying attention to the small details, knowing an individual customer's needs and preferences, and always searching for a way to improve the performance of your service or quality of your products. It's a guarantee that if you make all of these criteria a must, your business will grow tremendously due to your customer's satisfaction being exceeded beyond the point of the bare minimum.

Invest in Opportunities

Are you familiar with the saying, "*You reap what you sow*"? It basically means that the actions you take in the present produce the reality you experience in the future. Taking this into account, you have to invest in the people, resources, or places that will help your business continue to grow on a consistent basis. There are too many entrepreneurs who don't understand the importance of continuously seeking the right opportunities that work to expand the reach of their business. You alone can't take your business from the computer in your bedroom into the homes of thousands, or if you're lucky millions of people. You'll need a solid network made up of other people who work to bring your vision into its full existence.

Opportunities come in many forms but they're always presented by other people. Business is the interaction of people working together to achieve a common goal. Therefore, if you make the potential of your business attractive, people will want to assist its development with the opportunities that facilitate the growth process. As an entrepreneur, the more strategic your connections, the greater the net worth of your network becomes.

Be careful though, because every opportunity presented to you shouldn't be invested into without doing thorough research. The wrong investment can set your business back

Law IV

for months or even years, which makes it more susceptible to failure. It's like mergers and acquisitions on a smaller scale but with the same level off impact once you approve of the deal being confirmed. Only proceed forward if it makes sense and strengthens your position in the marketplace.

When it comes to finding opportunities, always think about how you can improve the performance of your business. Wherever your weaknesses are seek different options to strengthen them so they don't become a liability that holds your business back. Furthermore, you need to keep improving your strengths so that you create a position of domination, making it hard for the competition to even touch the advantage you control. Business is cut-throat and being an entrepreneur is equivalent to being a hunter. If you're not constantly on the prowl searching for the opportunity that will lead to a large feast, then you'll eventually starve fighting for the small scraps that are left over.

Law V

Law V: Your Reputation is Your Lifeline

There's no such thing as a self-made person. Even if you work extremely hard and make numerous personal sacrifices, your journey towards succeeds needs the assistance of other people to gain access you couldn't get on your own. The validation that a successful person grants you indicates to the public that you're among the very best -- the crème de la crème of providers. An industry authority vouching for you is a huge favor because they're risking their good name by promoting you to their followers who trust their opinion. They're putting their reputation on the line to help you build up your own.

Reputation is defined as beliefs or opinions held about someone or something. This means people form their own thoughts about your business based upon what they experience on a firsthand basis and through the secondhand accounts communicated by others. This is why a review site such as Yelp and Google reviews are very important to businesses. The opinions that patrons of your business communicate to the world can make or break you. Therefore, you have to control the perception that's held about your business by controlling the narrative.

You're the living embodiment of your business. Your own reputation is a direct reflection of how people will view your business. Good reputation, your business thrives. Bad reputation, people have second thoughts before handing you their money. This is why the board of Uber ousted Travis Kalanick out of the company he founded. The bad publicity that he was receiving on what seemed like every other week had a negative effect on the company's ability to retain customers and acquire new ones. He had to resign from his position as Uber's CEO before his growing bad reputation dug the company into a hole it couldn't possibly find its way out of.

If you're viewed as a toxic person, people are going to assume your business operates in the same manner. No sane person would want to waste their money on a business whose owner can't even be trusted. The perception that is formed in their mind is that you'll steal their money or sell them some crappy product. Therefore, they'll avoid doing business with you if it means having a peace of mind instead of dealing with your bullshit.

Perception creates the reality people see no matter if it's false. Luckily for you, you don't have to be a master manipulator to dictate how people perceive you and your business. Doing things the right way will make a far bigger impact than trying to operate upon a lie that will eventually unravel to expose your deception.

Avoid Scams and Quick Money Schemes

It's tempting to want to make big money in a very short period of time but the short-term reward is not worth the long-term ridicule you'll endure. There's no short-cut to wealth unless you get lucky and hit the lottery or are left a large inheritance. More often than not, though these people will lose the money they are given because it was not gained through discipline and sacrifice. What's easily gained tends to be easily lost. The same applies to money you swindle from people to live a lifestyle you haven't earned through hard work.

Devious individuals are always coming up with schemes to take advantage of people's eagerness to become an entrepreneur. This is because entrepreneurship has become synonymous with wealth and freedom, which is something people desperately want in a world that resembles a big rat race. Living paycheck to paycheck isn't fun and can cause great bouts of anxiety and deep depression. This is why you're always going to find individuals who are trying to find the best opportunity that will help them quickly escape such a bleak reality.

These type of circumstance can be looked at in two ways. You can either create a valuable product or service that actually helps people in these situations transition their life into a better existence. Or you can add to their misery by stealing the little money they do have because they were an easy target. You have some people who see the second option as the best choice and will construct elaborate cons to make a large amount of money in a very short amount of time. And while things are great in the beginning, the lie eventually unravels and you're left trying to create a believable lie to dissuade people from suing you or kicking your ass. All the confusion and legal issues that are a result of your scam aren't worth the ill gotten gains because the setbacks you incur will heavily outweigh the money you've stolen.

Take Bernie Madoff as an example of what happens when you create an extravagant scam that gets out of hand. Madoff lost $65,000,000,000 through his investment scam that went

Law V

on for nearly five decades. According to Madoff, everyday he felt like someone would finally uncover his scam. The pressure of keeping it up was very intense and he felt a sense of relief once he was finally caught and having to keep up the scam was over. For his fraudulent efforts, Madoff had his assets liquidated and was sentenced to 150 years in prison.

Before you put that work from home scam into motion think about how far it'll set you back in both your personal and business life. No one will ever trust you again and you'll have to start all over in a new location very far from where your last scam occurred. But you must remember we live in the age of social media. Whatever you do spreads quickly on places like Facebook and Instagram. So the ability to scam people in one location and moving to the next place to perpetuate your fraudulent activities is becoming very hard to do.

People Talk & Remember

While you're in the process of convincing a prospect to make a purchase, they're on Google trying to find out all they can about you. Any negative comments will cause them to hesitate about making the purchase, denying you the ability to make the sale and earn revenue for your business. You can try to explain what the cause is for the negative feedback but 9 times out of 10 that person has already crossed your business out of their mind as a legitimate provider.

There's no such thing as being perfect, especially when taking into account that some people can never be satisfied. But you have to be damn near perfect if you want to build a business that customers want to patronize on a regular basis.

Law V

You gain this type of attraction by ensuring that every interaction between customers and your business (you) is nothing less than professional. This can be hard to do on a consistent basis considering that some individuals like to be an ass for purely petty reasons. Being an entrepreneur though, means you must hold yourself to a standard higher than that of an idiot if you don't want your business to be given the label of having bad customer service. After all, you need customers to spend their money with your business on a consistent basis in order to grow into a dominant company within your industry.

You'll notice that the most successful companies always pay attention to what customers are saying about them and work to steer any negative comments towards having a conversation that leads to a positive resolution. It's all about being as proactive as you can be rather than being reactive. You do this by asking your customers questions about what you're doing well and where improvement can be made. This shows that you care about providing your customers with the best experience possible which they'll certainly appreciate.

When you have to be reactive, make sure that you always approach the situation with a win-win outcome in mind rather than preparing for a volatile confrontation. The tone you set usually dictates how the conversation will play out. As mentioned, there are rare cases when an individual wants to make you miserable just because they want to share their misery with others. Instead of stooping to their level; remain courteous, document what was said, and blacklist them from being a customer of your business again. When they try to slander your business's name, you'll be able to disprove their

Law V

claims with actual proof of the interaction between you and them. Taking this proactive route allows you to come out with a win when you're forced to be reactive.

The phrase *the customer is always right* isn't true but you must learn how to make them believe they're right. Due to social media being a big part of people's lives, how you respond to a customer is under a constant microscope. Even when you're not wrong, if a customer makes a public complaint, you need to make a public apology. Along with the apology, publically invite them to speak offline to handle the problem privately. By doing this you take control of the situation and sway public opinion in your favor by showing you work to solve any customer's issues they have with your business. This allows you to manage the perception of your business that you want acknowledged by the public.

Word of Mouth will Make or Break You

Word of mouth is so sacred for customers because it's conformation coming from someone they trust or an individual with first-hand experience of the business they're researching. Therefore, word of mouth is viewed in high regards because people trust an existing customer more than they do a business owner trying to convert them into a customer. This is why every interaction you have with both customers and prospects is very important. You're operating in the public realm where every word you say and action you take is being critiqued.

Customer validation is critical to the success of your business. Positive conversation about your business spreading on social media, being had at networking events,

52

and dominating the marketplace is a signal that your business should be viewed with favorable consideration. People have a tendency to want to be a part of the collective group when the members are enthusiastic about the great experience they're having. When enthusiasm for your business spreads like wildfire, it helps it grow exponentially because more and more people are being attracted due to great word of mouth.

As quickly as word of mouth can build your business up, it can also break it down until it's no longer able to operate at a viable level. Customer disapproval is very, very hard to turn around due to the power of perception. Too many negative conversations pertaining to how you operate your business and the inferior product or service you offer in the marketplace will make it impossible for you to establish a solid customer base. Bad word of mouth is basically a warning for other potential customers to stay very far away from your business. When you are dealing with this type of public disapproval you have two decisions to make: shut your business down and start over or hire an Olivia Pope who can effectively fix your image crisis.

How Will the Decision Affect You Long-Term?

A decision made never happens without a result being produced from the actions you take. This is why the saying, *think about the consequences of your actions* is very correct. You'll always have a lot of thoughts running through your mind concerning your business. The hard part about this is discerning which thoughts to proceed with and determining which are nothing but emotional impulses. Then you must also learn the fine line between making hasty decisions and procrastinating to avoid having to make them. Either of these responses being taken during your thought process can lead to consequences that could have easily been avoided with a thorough but decisive decision being made.

Entrepreneurship is about playing the long game. Even though you want immediate results in a fairly short amount of time, operating in this manner usually leads to short-cuts being taken. While you may get some results from taking this route, it never last long, leaving you panicking and scrambling to get something else going. Even though progress needs to consistently be made in the short-term, those gains need to align with your long-term plan. When this alignment occurs, your actions have deeper impact and your business builds a strong foundation that affords you some freedom in the marketplace to take some risks.

You must also remember you're an extension of your business. Even though you try to separate your personal life from your business life, it's hard to do so and most customers won't be able to make the distinction. This is why when a founder of a company gets in trouble in their personal life, their board typically pushes them out of the company before they drag the business institution down with them.

If your business isn't big enough to have a board to distinguish you from the organization, you can do serious damage to it when your personal issues become hard for the public to ignore. Therefore, you need to be accountable for your actions. More is expected of an entrepreneur, which is why you can't think or operate like the average person whose decisions are based on how they feel in the moment.

Law V

A decision made in the matter of seconds can destroy your personal brand and your business. Until you have *f##k you money* in your bank account, you have to be calculated about what you do. Your goal is to build an empire and empires aren't built by people who constantly make stupid decisions based on impulses. You have to think smart and perform with ruthless efficiency to transform your small business into a dominant market force that last for years to come.

Law VI

Law VI: Seek Wise Council

Entrepreneurship is a constant process of learning. You're going to make mistakes but those errors can be significantly reduced when you allow yourself to be open to learning from others. It's quite amazing how many entrepreneurs are so prideful that they're willing to stall their growth because they want to do everything by themselves. The reason behind such foolishness is to say they did it 'all on their own' -- a real "self-made" story. This is ignorant thinking because every successful entrepreneur you look up to had some type of help from other people to turn their raw potential into greatness. Whether it's to gain connections, knowledge, or monetary investment; you have to get other people involved with your business to bring it into fruition and ensure that it flourishes beyond a year or two.

Get a Mentor

There's no better teacher than experience. Experience is gained from going through the process of trial and error but this method of learning can lead to slow growth. To cut your learning curve in half it's better to learn from the individuals who have achieved what you're seeking to accomplish for yourself. Their advice and mentorship can help you see things that were closed off in your mind due to your inexperience about building a business. When you match wisdom with hustle and ambition, extraordinary feats can be accomplished.

It's important that you find the right mentor(s) who can get the best out of you. Your personalities have to be in sync in order to have a great relationship that serves you both well.

Law VI

Just as you learn from your mentor they can also learn from you because you're working to bring innovation to your industry. You can open their eyes to new ways of thinking, while they direct you towards the people and resources that can enable you to continue to grow your business beyond where you can take it on your own.

A mentor has to see something special in you to be willing to help guide your entrepreneurial journey. Imagine how many other people are trying to get their attention so they can be their mentee. You have to standout by not only showing how hungry you are but by showing you have a promising business that has potential to succeed. If a person is giving up their time to mentor you, they want some surety that they're backing a winner. It's an absolute waste of their time to be spent on someone who'll come up short because they don't possess that extra push that is needed to be successful.

The greats learn from the greats. If your goal is to be a successful entrepreneur, you first need to learn how to think and operate like a seasoned entrepreneur. Even when you eventually gain the success you desire, it doesn't mean that you can't continue leaning on mentors for their wisdom and experience. Great entrepreneurs see themselves as lifelong students who always need to be educated in order to increase the power of their minds.

If you're a six figure earner, you want to learn from your millionaire mentor how to make $1,000,000. When you become a millionaire, you want to learn from your billionaire mentor how to make $1,000,000,000. There's always something new to learn in entrepreneurship and you need to

Law VI

constantly seek out those who can provide you with the knowledge you don't have so you can continually improve.

Surround Yourself with Your Weaknesses

The problem that many entrepreneurs have is their pride and huge ego. They choose to go the solitary route to prove their intelligence and work-ethic but it tends to backfire on them. This is because everyone in the world has weaknesses that coincide with their strengths. Even though you can rely on your strengths to propel you forward, your weaknesses will eventually catch up to you when faced with situations where they need to be relied upon. You then place yourself in a precarious predicament because you chose to operate as a one man army and you don't have anyone else to rely on to help you out.

Intelligent entrepreneurs understand where they excel and where their abilities are lacking. When you know your deficiencies, you can offset them by bringing in people whose strengths are your weaknesses. Success is all about positioning and knowing how to improve yours in order to accomplish the goals you have set to be achieved. It's not weak to say you need help when that support can lead to your business becoming a multi-million dollar operation. It basically comes down to the choice of struggling by yourself or improving with the help of others.

You probably read Forbes, Entrepreneur, Inc, or one of those other magazines that discuss the entrepreneurial process and individual success stories. These publications are successful among entrepreneurs but their founders don't write every single story. They have a team of writers who create

Law VI

hundreds of pieces of content on a daily basis so their websites are continuously updated to keep readers coming back for more. The pieces (writers) work to propel the whole (publication) so that it remains successful, especially when they use its authority as a vehicle for their own success on an individual level.

The founders of PayPal, often referred to as the PayPal Mafia, were a group of individuals with distinct skill sets who came together to make the company a game changer in the financial marketplace. What is considered as one of the first fintech companies, the disruption caused by PayPal in the financial industry wouldn't have occurred without these individuals recognizing the importance of combining the strengths of other intelligent people to build an innovative company. Doing this not only taught them how to work with other alpha entrepreneurs but they also learned what it took to create their own billion dollar companies that would later transform other industries.

This is why you must apply this type of thinking to your own entrepreneurial aspirations if you want to reach the very top. There's power in numbers but you have to be strategic about who you place around you to help assist in your entrepreneurial journey. Just because you need help it doesn't mean that you just bring on anyone without verifying their qualifications. People will lie about their abilities to only set your business back with their inability to get the job done you have brought them on to do. You're basically increasing the impact of your weaknesses when this occurs, which makes it impossible to succeed.

Law VI

Delegate as Much as Possible

The importance of recognizing your core strengths is you know what to focus on and what to allow others to handle for you. If you're great at selling then you should put all your energy into selling instead of wasting time on administrative tasks. Your responsibility is to invest your time and energy into the role that will lead to your business growing. When you venture outside of that role, you're only hurting the ability for your company to be successful. Therefore, you must learn how to get out of the way instead of hindering your business's performance.

You get more done when you give other people key responsibilities instead of trying to carry the entire load on your shoulders. It's already a difficult task to build a business but you make it impossible when you're trying to do everyone else's job along with steering your organization in the right direction. Your focus becomes fragmented, which means your efficiency drops, and you start to lose control of your business. But you become so distracted by the confusion of trying to do everything on your own that you don't realize your business is declining as each day passes.

It makes no sense to be one of those owners who delegates tasks but still micromanages the entire process. This means that you don't trust the people you have brought into your business to help it grow. If this is the mindset you possess, you alienate your team because they feel that you don't believe in them. In turn they rebel against you to create the independence they seek.

Law VI

All successful teams, organizations, and businesses know the that role each member plays, so there is no interference with an individual's work process. Beyond assisting them when support is needed to complete their job, each individual on your team wants to feel like they're actually contributing to the success of your business. Allow the members on your team to function in their roles without your constant meddling so that they can learn and grow to become a greater asset for your company.

Law VII

Law VII: Diversify Your Core Business

When you create a position of dependency, you put yourself at a disadvantage that tends to bite you at the most unexpected times. Having one source of revenue is very dangerous. Matter of fact, it should be criminal for an entrepreneur to operate a business that only makes money doing one specific thing. No moment is guaranteed to remain the same way in your personal life and the same goes for the performance of your business. If your business's income is dependent on only one monetary generator, your financial stability is always going to be uncertain.

Companies like Macys, JcPennys, and Sears were dependent on one demographic -- the middle class. When the middle class's income started to decline, these stores saw their sales decline as a result. Believing that the middle class would only continue to grow made these companies vulnerable to the financial struggles and eventual disappearance of this social class. Now these companies are struggling to attract new customers, having to shut down many of their stores because they're no longer assets, only money draining liabilities.

Think of your business as a living body. Your body needs many different types of nutrients to survive and function properly. If you decided to only eat only one type of food, your body will eventually break down because you're ignoring the other important food sources your body needs to perform effectively. The same thing occurs when your business only has one revenue source driving its growth. If that money flow stops, your company dies because it's

Law VII

being deprived the blood flow every business needs to live--sales.

How to Make $1 Four Different Ways

It's been stated that a millionaire has seven different sources of income. The reason behind this strategy is because money is fickle. One minute it loves you and the next minute it deserts you. To keep its attention you need to give it many different options where it can be entertained and work. And when your money works for you, you're no longer struggling to keep it attracted to you.

To show you how this work, let's use the example of a consultant. Everyone is a consultant these days trying to sell their experience and knowledge. The problem many consultants deal with, though is attracting clients and learning how to make money outside of one-on-one consulting. This makes them desperate for clients and you typically see them almost begging for new business via social media by lowering their prices.

The issue lies with the fact that they're putting too much into consulting, instead of focusing on their communicating their value in multiple ways. When you're selling knowledge, it can be packaged in many different ways to be purchased. This packaging includes: classes/ training, books, and webinars. You use these different vehicles of communication to make money, while marketing the full course meal of your consulting services. People who attend your classes may choose to become a client if you taught them something new. Readers of your book may choose to become a client if the material you wrote helped them see their problem from a

Law VII

different perspective. You're still getting paid while enticing people to take the final step towards becoming a consulting client. It's a win-win strategy that allows you to make money even when your main pipeline is dry at the moment.

Now imagine if all your income pipelines were full at the same time during the second quarter of the year. You'd be making so much money during that busy period that a slow month later in the year wouldn't put you in the financial strain that would occur if you only had one source of income. This is why it's very important to stop thinking of money in a linear manner and instead view it flowing in a circular motion. When this is how you see money, you understand you need multiple things flowing at the same time to complete the circle.

What Opportunities are You Missing?

You will always miss opportunities that are available to you when your eyes are closed to them. Apple started off as a computer company and today has expanded into phones, the creative industry (iMac = music and movies), and television. Taking the risk to pursue other opportunities helped the company to grow into a nearly trillion dollar company today. This wouldn't have been possible without Steve Jobs seeking new ways to grow the Apple brand beyond its then current status.

Think about the ways you can innovate your business to operate in new marketplaces to attract new customers. Not only are you making more money but you're building a stronger brand. Brand recognition is an asset that provides you with opportunities unknown companies will never be

64

Law VII

able to attract. But this access is only granted to you when you push your business beyond its initial boundaries. Sometimes you have to take the path not guaranteed to be successful in order to experience the wild success that comes with taking a big risk.

If you put out that book you've been procrastinating writing it could lead to speaking engagements, television interviews, and authority status in your industry. That training program you keep on your desk could be implemented by corporations, leading to you gaining corporate clients who pay extremely well. You'll continue to miss the big opportunities if you're afraid to take your shot. It doesn't matter if you miss on your first couple (or hundreds) of attempts. The one shot you do make can be the winning basket that leads to a string of victories.

Creating Market Domination

Apple, Amazon, Google, Facebook, and Nike are all dominate companies that own the industries they operate within. How they established such control is by creating a product or service people had to have and then investing in other complementary assets that would further expand their dominate position. The goal is to experience continual upward mobility instead of maintaining a stagnant position of average existence.

The first step towards market domination is creating a valuable product or service that has very high demand. You then keep developing new offers that keep your customers excited with anticipation for what you're working on next. This is how you keep interest in your company alive so that

your supply is continually met with demand. The more
money you make leads to you being able to invest in product
development, acquisitions, and operations in different
industries. These type of moves transition you from a small
business operation into an international corporation.

Being strategic and having patience are two of the most
important qualities you must have when seeking to become a
market leader. If you rush then you make sloppy mistakes. If
you don't have a plan of action then you can't produce
consistent results. To be the best comes with a lot of
challenges and dealing with trial and errors. But you can't
pass up the opportunity to gain increased positioning when
it's there for you to grab. It's all about how bad you want to
be recognized as the top dog in your industry.

Law VIII

Law VIII: Gain Authority & Influence

The words authority and influence are synonymous with success. The ability to captivate people and have them follow your lead is developed when you can demonstrate your value to the world. You have to give people a reason to believe in you so that they can be inspired by your presence, words, and actions. Become a magnetic force that draws people in with your passion and ideas. The ambition that you have and your drive to be the best will make people want to support you and see to it that you gain even more success.

The individuals who have large followings and die-hard supporters are those who believed they had something great that needed to be shared with others. Instead of hiding their talents, they broadcasted them so that people understood the extraordinary gifts they possessed. They worked hard to put themselves in the position to be seen and heard. Remaining in mediocrity was no longer an option that would be accepted by them. The only option was to go all in and bet on themselves to see how far they could climb up the ladder of success.

The success of your business is dependent on how far you can take it. In today's world, your personal brand is just as important as your business's brand. Customers want to know what makes you great and how that translates to the value provided by your business. You and your business are bound together like a marriage. Therefore, you have to represent it well to ensure that the marriage remains blissful and grows stronger every day.

Law VIII

There's no way you can compete with established business's without building your authority. Authority status is based on trust and proven results. You must prove both to build up your name and attract a strong following of loyal supporters. The more people you have validating you and praising your work leads to even more people seeking you out to see how you can improve their business or personal life. It soon gets to the point where you're so overwhelmed with demand that you have to turn people away so that you can properly take care of your current clients. This image looks great in your head while reading these combination of words but you must actually seek to become an authority instead of merely daydreaming about being one.

Develop Your Brand

Your brand is very important because it's a representation of your business. It's how people identify your company before its name is even spoken. When you see the bitten apple, you know its Apple. When you see the golden arches, you know its McDonalds. When you see the swoosh (check mark), you know its Nike. These are branding logos that are worth billions of dollars that took decades to build up their recognition. Although, you might have a business logo that definitely needs to become your company's brand symbol, your brand needs to be developed from your story.

Your business was created to serve a need so you must communicate this to your audience on a consistent basis. Tell them the problem you saw that existed. Share how you sought out to create the solution that would eradicate that problem. Make them realize that you're an unique individual who wants to help them and the value that you placed into you products or services is something they can't ignore and must have. Your goal is to craft a compelling story that people want to be a part of themselves.

Michael Jordan is a brand, recognized as the best basketball player that ever lived. Before Nike made the mistake of saturating the marketplace with his shoes, people would camp out for days when his shoes were going to be released to purchase a pair. Jordan himself can be given partial credit for why this occurred but it was the exclusivity of owning a pair of shoes everyone else wanted but didn't have the chance to purchase, is what drove the frenzy for Air Jordans. Once again, it's all about perception. It's the same thing that Apple does when they release a new iPhone. Owning these products means that you're among an exclusive group that everyone can't be a part of but wish they were.

The narration of your brand's story leads to the development of your products and services value. It's not simply about saying you're the best. You have to lay out the case for why you're the best while explaining it through the eyes of the customer. Because at the end of the day, all they want to know is how are you going to make their life better. Make that fact known and you won't have any trouble building the strength and recognition of your brand.

Seek Exposure

Closed mouths don't get fed and unknown individuals don't get paid. It doesn't matter how intelligent you are, how hard you work, and how "deserving" of success you believe you are. If people aren't aware of your existence then you get overlooked an individual with better recognition. All that complaining about others experiencing more success than you, while not actually being better than you is a waste of time. Constantly get in the face of your audience so that they can become aware of the value you offer. With a consistent effort, you'll eventually be seen and heard and will gain an audience who enjoys your content.

There's too many avenues to gain exposure in today's world. People are using platforms like blogging, YouTube, and Instagram to build up their audience, which provides them with bigger opportunities as their popularity continues growing. Even if half of these individuals aren't even that talented, the quality they do posses is hustle. When you hustle and are persistent, you'll eventually find some type of success because the law of attraction can't deny your work ethic. The more that people consistently see your content on these different platforms, they have to start paying attention to you because they can see you're serious about whatever it is you're doing.

Beyond social media, you need to gain exposure on authority platforms. These are the websites, blogs, podcast, and internet shows that your target audience frequents to learn about the particular problems your business solves. If you want immediate validation, you need to frequently appear on these different platforms discussing your story and demonstrating your knowledge about your industry. This is one of the best ways to develop trust because other authorities allowing you to share their space says that you're legit. This eases any reservations they would have if they were just going off of your own appeal for why they need to buy into you.

Law VIII

You might be tempted to do something controversial to get noticed because controversy gets people talking but think about it before taking this route. Your brand is the representation of your business so the actions you take and the words and images you put in the atmosphere are a representation of your brand. So if you want to do something shocking just to get people's attention, you could possibly do serious damage to your brand that people will always remember (remember that thing called social media?).

The NFL had an example of brand controversy with the players kneeling during the national anthem. Half of the country is against this type of protest, which has not only harmed the NFL brand but also supposedly the sponsors' brands who support the sports association. Papa John's Pizza released a statement calling out the NFL about their lack of leadership for allowing these protest and the perceived disrespect players were showing for the United State's flag. Papa John's then had Neo-Nazis supporting their stance, which the company strongly tried to distance itself from to not be labeled a racist company. The cautionary tale from this mess is that you need to control all elements of your brand. If you create a story that gets out of your control, you put your brand in a negative position that could be hard to pivot out of.

Piggy Back of Other's Authority

Even though you learn important lessons while in the building process, you don't want to deal with slow paced growth for a very long time. But when you're building up your authority, it takes quite a while to get the attention of your target audience because they're focused on the

Law VIII

established authorities in your industry. You can either choose to do the slow grind and build up your authority over an extended period of time (a year or two) or you can use the established authority of your counterparts to help you build your own a little quicker.

How this works is getting these individuals to promote you to their audience. But this is not just free promotion to help you. There needs to be a mutual exchange of benefit that occurs, whether it be monetary, a partnership, or giving them the opportunity to be in front of your audience (now or in the future). The best time to do this is when you have a new book to promote or a product or service that you're about to release. But think ahead about establishing this relationship with their audience. Before you even begin to sell your offer, create content that warms their audience up to you. The familiarity will be there and they'll have knowledge beforehand about who you are and what you represent when you do decide to offer them a product to purchase.

You might think this is asking too much of people who already have the success you desire but that's definitely not true. They started off from nothing just like you and know how hard it can be establishing your place among a crowded field of competitors. If they see that you're working your ass off and have real value to contribute to the marketplace, they'll have no problem giving you some exposure to increase awareness about your expertise and the value you offer.

Law VIII

Remain Relevant

The hardest part about success is the demand it takes to remain successful. There are people who are fighting for the attention of the same audience you're focused on. If your consistency starts to lag and your content quality starts to suffer, you'll lose the influence you've work hard to build up. That would be terrible because when your influence decreases, your money tends to constrict as a result. All this because you got comfortable and lazy, thinking that your long-term success was guaranteed because your audience 'loves you'.

You must stay creating authoritative content, writing new books, developing valuable products, and adding on to your existing services to remain relevant. The law of success demands that you continuously work hard or you must make room for someone else who wants the position you hold. You have to keep giving people a reason to pay attention to you because they're already fickle in the first place. Therefore, you have to earn their support on a continual basis in order for them to acknowledge your position as an authority on a long-term basis.

Tony Robbins has been the top authority in the coaching industry for decades. The reason so is because he keeps releasing new material and bringing attention to the effectiveness of his methods. In order to hold your dominate position you have to remind people about just how great you are. Don't look at it as bragging or attention whoring. It's all about ensuring you preserve your brand's power and maintain the influence that you worked so hard to earn.

Law IX

Law IX: View Money as a Means to Freedom

Foolish people say that money is the root of all evil. While it's true that worshiping money can corrupt your mind, the access granted by having money is lovely. No one enjoys the misery of struggling. When you're in a financially dire situation, your mind is constantly wondering about how great it would be to be wealthy or even financially comfortable. This is because having no money denies your ability to fully enjoy life. Sure, people say having your health and family around means you have a wealthy life but that's just a colorful way to say you're okay with being at the bottom. If you have a family, you should demand more from yourself so that you can provide them with the best the world has to offer. And the only way this is possible is when you're financially secure.

The important thing to understand when it comes to money is that it's just paper. When you chase the paper you always come up empty handed because it has no real value. What you really need to be focused on is serving a need with a great product or service that's valued in the marketplace. When you do this money becomes attracted to you because you're more concerned with solving a problem with an effective solution rather than chasing the trappings of money.

Money is nothing more than a tool that can be used to build your life up. While it's important in that regards, never allow it to control you. It may seem hard to grasp that concept when it's being said that money has no value, but at the same time it does grant freedom. To help you better understand

74

Law IX

this logic look at it from the following perspective. Money represents the perceived value provided by a person, place, or thing. You're not placing any value in money per se. What you're actually doing is saying the commodity that you want is valuable to you for whatever the reason may be. Therefore, you value a peace of mind, new experiences, and exclusive access. These desires are only afforded to you when you have the money to validate your ability to possess them. This means you exchange your knowledge or products in exchange for the tangible piece of paper called money

We live in a world today where there's barely any financial middle ground anymore. You're either wealthy or you're the working poor. Going to a job for 40 or more hours a week to just get a check that is used to pay bills and participate in a little consumerism defines you as the working poor. When you're financing your personal expenses with debt, you're the working poor. To get out of this misery you need to learn how to generate money in large sums and use it as a tool to obtain real freedom in the world.

Sales & Profit

The only way you can build a successful business is when your product and services are being sold on a consistent basis. Without sales occurring you have no business. You're just wasting your time trying to appear like an entrepreneur instead of actually hustling like an entrepreneur. All those social media post, networking events, and 'meetings' mean nothing if they're not leading to your products or services being sold. The sales process should be your main concern every single day because sales is the blood of your business.

Law IX

Once that blood flow stops, your business is dead because no money is being circulated through it to keep it functioning.

The main criteria that allows you to generate sales is being able to communicate and validate the value of your products and services. This makes the sales process easier because you're educating the prospect instead of selling to them. The difference between the two is identifying the key reasons why they need to become your customer based on their particular needs, rather than forcing the sale by talking about how great your offer is. When you make the focus about the prospect, they can better visualize how your solution will resolve their current problems and allow them to produce better results. When you make the focus about you, they tune you out because you're not addressing their needs, which in their mind means you can't possibly help them.

Once you get a better grasp of selling, you must understand revenue and expenses. The more money it cost you to operate your business, the less money you have staying within your company bank account. You could be generating $1,000,000 in revenue a year but only have $5,000 or a negative balance at the end of the year because your expenses are outrageously high. Most business owners don't typically notice this deficit until it's too late and then they're left clueless about where all their money is going. In their mind $1,000,000 in revenue is equivalent to money they have. They don't know the difference between revenue and profit until they're shocked by the lack of money they actually have.

To earn a profit in your business you need to make sure your expenses don't exceed your revenue. Profit is what you use to grow your business, invest in other opportunities and even pay yourself more if it's feasible. When your business isn't generating a profit, it either means your sales aren't strong enough or your expenses are too high. You need to find out what the issue is so that you can take the necessary actions to make your business healthier. This is why CEOs of large corporations lay off thousands of workers when the company is underperforming financially. They need to make a profit to pay the shareholders whose money was used to finance the growth the corporation. It might seem like an asshole move but their main concern is keeping their shareholders happy so they don't lose their support and lose their job. Likewise, you'll eventually lose your own business if you're not actually making money on your sales by keeping your business lean and growing your customer base.

Make Your Money Work for You

Once you start generating a solid income you need to reverse the roles between you and money. You've worked your ass off to make the money you've earned and you'll continue doing so in the future until you reach your number (**f**k you money in the bank**), if you have one. But as you're continuing to hustle and build, your money needs to be doing the same thing simultaneously so that the return for your efforts are exponentially increased. When you make money follow your lead, it produces higher returns than what you could possibly do on your own without it's assistance. But you have to understand how to guide your money in the right direction so that it multiplies rather than fleeing your grasp.

Investing is the best way to put your money to work. The investing opportunities include real estate, stocks, startups, and existing businesses. What you must do is find the best opportunity available to you at a price point you're comfortable with losing in case the investment ends up going under. This is why you should spread your investments so that you have a better chance of increasing your odds of success. If you happen to get lucky and find a passive income stream where the investment increases exponentially due to market demand, you've now increased your wealth without having to be actively involved in that money generating process. Capitalism is quite beautiful when you're able to really participate within it!

You've heard the quote, "make money in your sleep", and became fascinated about doing this yourself. When you invest in business automation and income generating assets this fascination becomes a reality. But this only happens when you view money as the tool for freedom it is and not as something you use solely for personal consumption. Because once the consumer mindset takes root in your mind, you hand back over the control to money and it dictates the rules in your relationship once again.

Enjoy Your Gains but Don't Splurge

It's difficult to not want to spend money on material things, especially after you worked your ass off to earn it. But you have to resist the urge to splurge if you want to maintain your wealth. Remember, your goal is to consistently increase your wealth, rather than constantly working to replace the money you spent. When you spend more money than you make, you're staying in the rat race because you're never in the position of being ahead. You have no discipline, which means you have no right to claim authority over the money you possess.

Law IX

There's no problem with spending money in moderation as long as it doesn't create financial distress. But when you're buying houses, cars, and other material things that you can't afford as their expenses accumulate, you're just being stupid. Enjoy your money because you worked hard for it but remain focused on your long-term financial goals and not your short-term pleasures. When your pleasures control your actions, you'll quickly find yourself trying to rebuild the business you once practiced discipline to build.

Law X

Law X: Have an Exit Strategy

When you create a business, your end-goal needs to be in mind from day one. This is the ultimate goal that drives you to take your business as far as you can take it before it's time to write a new chapter in your entrepreneurial life. Your exit strategy helps you create the vision for your business and implement the strategy you'll utilize to accomplish your goals. This helps you remain focused and determine how to change your approach in case you're not meeting the targets that have been set to be achieved by a certain time frame.

It might seem odd to be thinking about your exit so soon but it's necessary to do if you want your business to grow quickly -- helping you to become financially successful at the same time. You're eliminating any possibility of having a lackadaisical approach and setting a fire under your ass to get shit done in a designated amount of time. You're working with calculated aggression instead of having a passive attitude that only stagnates your business's growth. With an exit strategy in place, you know what phase you're in when it comes to your personal relationship with your business as you come closer to reaching the end goal.

What was Your Goal When Starting?

There's a reason you started your business and pushed to ensure it grew consistently. Maybe your goal is to sell your business for $10,000,000, pass it on to your kids, or take it public. Whatever it is, you need to approach every single day with that end-goal in mind so that it pushes you to give 100% effort every day. When you're guided by motivation, it forces you to overcome challenges and think outside the box to

Law X

secure the prize your desire. You'll work hard to position yourself for the win rather than being satisfied with coming up short. You can't afford to not win because everything you did would have just been a waste of time if your goal isn't accomplished. This is the mindset athletes hold when they don't win a championship, which drives them to work harder until they're finally crowned a champion. All accomplishments mean nothing if you can't say that you achieved the ultimate goal you were after.

You have to determine how bad you want to accomplish your goal. It's about holding yourself accountable to the promise you made to yourself to be successful no matter what. Getting halfway there isn't considered a success. The outside world may view your accomplishments as success but you know that's not true because you didn't complete what you set out to do. You must be accountable for your words and ensure that your actions bring them into fruition.

Many successful entrepreneurs use affirmations to guide the actions of their day. By affirming to themselves their goals and what they'll do to accomplish them, they make the achievement of their goals an obsession. The use of affirmations is a constant reminder to yourself that you'll only achieve greatness when your thoughts and actions are a reflection of being great. Never allow yourself to settle for less and constantly push yourself to conquer any challenge you face by possessing the thoughts and actions that help you dominate your goals.

Law X

What Makes You Happy?

Your entrepreneurial journey should not only be about serving the needs of others but also about earning the life that makes you happy. You're working hard to gain real financial freedom in a world where so many people are miserable with their existence. But you have chosen to not merely exist. You want to live and thrive so that you have full access to what the world has to offer. You don't want to hold yourself back and be full of regrets when you look back on what you didn't accomplish in your life. You chose the path of entrepreneurship because you decided to take control of your life so that you're the only one who dictates how your story will be remembered.

Mediocrity and living paycheck to paycheck is not life -- it's a living hell. But you will remain in this purgatory if you don't set out to change the course of your life. The entrepreneurial path isn't easy but what's worth having is never earned with ease. You'll work incredibly hard to climb the ladder of success but earning it will bring you happiness knowing how far away you're removed from the low position you were once at.

Many people will read this book but only a few will actually seek to make a change in their thoughts and behavior to become successful. I hope I will have to take this statement back, though because I want all readers of this book to succeed. There's plenty of opportunity out here to be successful but how bad do you want it?